| DATE DUE | | | |
|---|---|---|---|
| FEB 13 | | | |
| FEB 20 | | | |
| FEB 28 | | | |
| MAR 6 | | | |
| MAR 14 | | | |
| MAR 15 | | | |
| | | | |
| | | | |
| | | | |
| | | | |
| | | | |

```
18886                              E
Yorke                              Y
Molly the mad basher.
```

**Woodridge Elementary Library**
**3313 Northampton Road**
**Cuyahoga Falls, Ohio 44223**

# MOLLY
## THE MAD BASHER

Malcolm Yorke
with illustrations by
Margaret Chamberlain

DORLING KINDERSLEY
LONDON • NEW YORK • STUTTGART

A DORLING KINDERSLEY BOOK

First American Edition, 1994
2 4 6 8 10 9 7 5 3 1

Published in the United States by
Dorling Kindersley, Inc., 232 Madison Avenue
New York, New York 10016

Copyright © 1994 Dorling Kindersley Limited, London
Text copyright © 1994 Malcolm Yorke
Illustrations copyright © 1994 Margaret Chamberlain

The author's moral rights have been asserted.

All rights reserved under International and Pan-American Copyright Conventions.
No part of this publication may be reproduced, stored in a retrieval system, or
transmitted in any form or by any means, electronic, mechanical, photocopying, recording,
or otherwise, without the prior written permission of the copyright owner.
Published in Great Britain by Dorling Kindersley Limited.
Distributed by Houghton Mifflin Company, Boston.

**Library of Congress Cataloging-in-Publication Data**
Yorke, Malcolm, 1938—Molly the Mad Basher / written by Malcolm Yorke;
illustrated by Margaret Chamberlain.
— 1st American ed.
p. cm. —
(Teachers' secrets) Summary: When Miss Molly Cuddle takes her class on a visit
to the new shopping center, the students discover their teacher's secret talents.
ISBN 1-56458-459-3
[1. Teachers—Fiction. 2. Wrestling—Fiction.
3. School field trips—Fiction. 4. Humorous stories.]
I. Chamberlain, Margaret, ill. II. Title. III. Series.
PZ7.Y8244Mo 1993              93-11407
[E]—dc20                         CIP
                                  AC

Color reproduction by DOT Gradations Ltd.
Printed in Singapore

Molly Cuddle is a teacher. Her students like her very much because she reads them great stories, they get to do lots of splashy painting, sing songs together, play recorders, and learn how things work.

• Teachers' Secrets •

Their classroom is always full of flowers and interesting things to smell or taste or play around with and take apart.

Nobody in Molly Cuddle's class is ever bored.

One Monday the class decided to do a research project about the new shopping center. You know the kind of thing. First they read the center's advertisements in the local newspaper. Next, Emma's group looked up the addresses in the phone book and wrote letters to the storekeepers asking if the class could come to visit them.

Then Ali's group worked out the best way to get there on the map, and Derek and Mai's group made a list of questions to ask their families and neighbors about the stores they used. They were very busy all day.

• MOLLY THE MAD BASHER •

Molly Cuddle went home rather tired, but very pleased with her class. She had a cup of tea and a muffin while she watched TV. Then she fed her old cat, Cuddlebum. At seven o' clock she packed a bag, got into her little car, and drove off to the nearby city.

• Teachers' Secrets •

She parked near the Sports Stadium and went around the back to the Women's Dressing Rooms. There she hung up her teaching clothes, took off her glasses, and put on a stretchy red unitard. Then she pulled on a pair of tall red boots.

Finally she covered every bit of her face with red face paint and drew on some terrible black eyebrows. She also wore a wild red wig. Across the back of her red unitard was printed in big letters: MOLLY THE MAD BASHER.

# MOLLY THE MAD BASHER

When her opponent, Pretty Polly, appeared on the opposite side of the stadium, the crowd cheered wildly, blowing kisses and singing.

FOR SHE'S A JOLLY GOOD LAY – YAY – DEE AND SO SAY ALL OF US!

# Teachers' Secrets

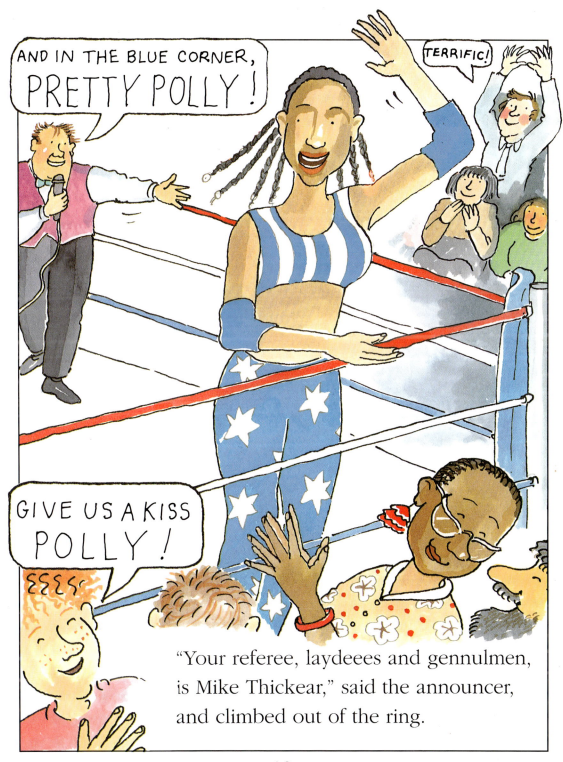

"Your referee, laydeees and gennulmen, is Mike Thickear," said the announcer, and climbed out of the ring.

• TEACHERS' SECRETS •

Clang! Round one!

Pretty Polly began by trying a half nelson, but the Basher wriggled free. She got Pretty Polly in a knee-press, then an airplane spin, and finally threw her right out of the ring into the second row of seats!

Round one to Molly the Mad Basher. The crowd booed and booed.

• MOLLY THE MAD BASHER •

Clang! Round two!

Pretty Polly drop-kicked the Basher, bounced her off the corner post, and sat on her head. The Basher bit Polly's bottom when the referee wasn't looking. But then Polly won the round with a great body-slam on the Basher.

Round two to Pretty Polly.

The crowd loved it and cheered and cheered.

Clang! Round three!

Polly put the Basher in a full-nelson lock and tried to screw the Basher's head right off her neck. But the Basher got her back with a pile-driver.

Round three to Molly the Mad Basher!

"Cheat! Rotten! Get lost, Basher! Boooooo!" howled the crowd.

# MOLLY THE MAD BASHER

Clang! Round four!

Next, they both leaped in feet first from their corners . . . and missed! The Basher's fist accidentally caught Mike Thickear on the jaw and he took a long time to recover. Then Polly got the Basher in a quick scissors, a flying mare, and a leg-stretch.

Round four to Pretty Polly.

The crowd whooped and whistled!

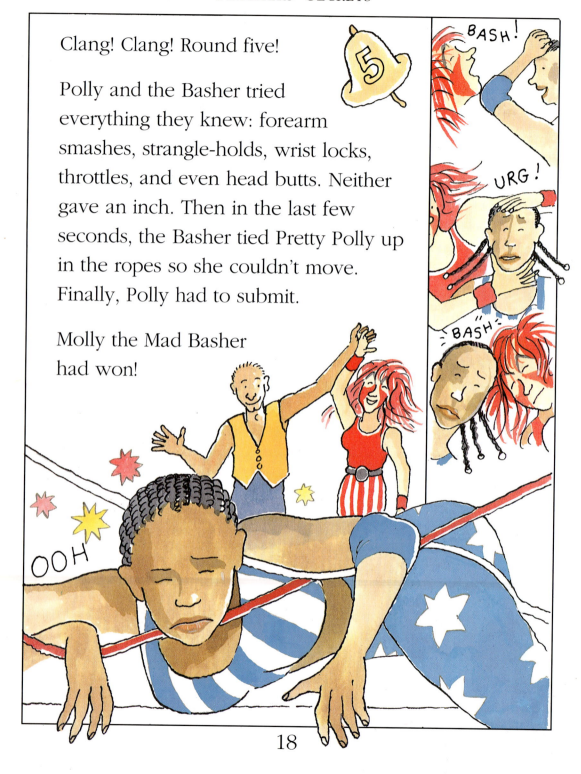

Clang! Clang! Round five!

Polly and the Basher tried everything they knew: forearm smashes, strangle-holds, wrist locks, throttles, and even head butts. Neither gave an inch. Then in the last few seconds, the Basher tied Pretty Polly up in the ropes so she couldn't move. Finally, Polly had to submit.

Molly the Mad Basher had won!

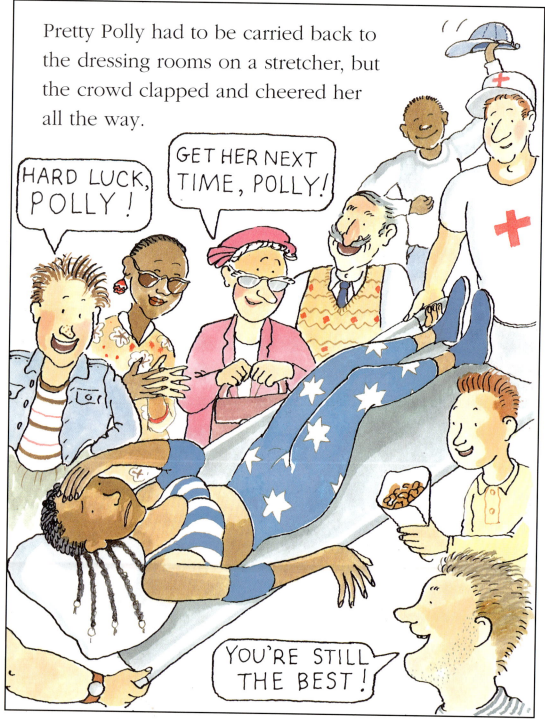

# MOLLY THE MAD BASHER

Molly the Mad Basher took off her face paint, her terrible eyebrows and wig, and became Molly Cuddle again. She showered, then ran around to the corner café for a cup of coffee and a piece of cake with her best friend.

It was Pretty Polly! Her real name was Polly Stibbs and she had only pretended to need a stretcher at the end of the bout. During the day, Polly worked in a beauty parlor.

"That was a great pile-driver in the third round, Molly," said Polly.

"Well, thank you, Polly. And that was an amazing throttle you used in the last round. You'll have to show me how you hold your fingers for that."

"I'd be glad to, Molly, but now I've got to hurry for the baby-sitter. I try to get back in time for the children's bedtime story."

"'Bye then, Polly. Your turn to win next week!" said Molly.

"'Bye Molly, thanks for the fun," said Polly, and away she went.

• Teachers' Secrets •

Molly Cuddle drove home. She ate a light supper, prepared her lessons for the next day, and went to bed tired and happy.

"Oh, I **do** like Mondays," she told Cuddlebum as she switched off the light.

• MOLLY THE MAD BASHER •

On Tuesday and Wednesday, the class continued to prepare for their visit to the shopping center. Emma's group made a plan of the center, ready to fill in the names of the stores. Mai's and Ali's groups made lists of questions to ask the shoppers and storekeepers. "Are there enough trash bins, restrooms, and fire exits? Can you get around in a wheelchair? What about seats for elderly people?"

They were all very busy and excited, including, of course, Molly Cuddle.

• Teachers' Secrets •

On Thursday, after homeroom, the class followed Molly Cuddle in an orderly line to the shopping center, talking excitedly as they went.

"Now, here we are. Notebooks and maps ready? Good," said Molly. "I think we'll begin with the jewelry store. Mr. MacSparkle is expecting us and we're exactly on . . ."

• MOLLY THE MAD BASHER •

At that very moment there was a scream, a shout, and a crash! Two big men burst out of the jewelry store, stuffing trays of rings and watches into bags as they ran. They knocked over several of the children and pushed an elderly lady roughly aside.

• Teachers' Secrets •

But when the first man tried to push Molly Cuddle aside, she punched him in the jaw. Then she tossed the second man over her shoulder, did a scissors on the first, threw the second into the fountain, and slammed the first head down into a trash bin.

# MOLLY THE MAD BASHER

Then she fished them out and tied their arms and legs together so tightly that they couldn't move a muscle. Mr. MacSparkle called the police.

Molly wasn't even out of breath—although she did have a run in her tights!

SPERLASH!

DUNK

# MOLLY THE MAD BASHER

"Wow! That was better than the wrestling on TV," said one of the crowd.

Can we help you with your project?" asked an elderly lady.

"First, let's all give three cheers for Miss Molly Cuddle: Hip-hip-hooray!"

"Well," thought Molly. "It **is** nice not to be booed for once!"

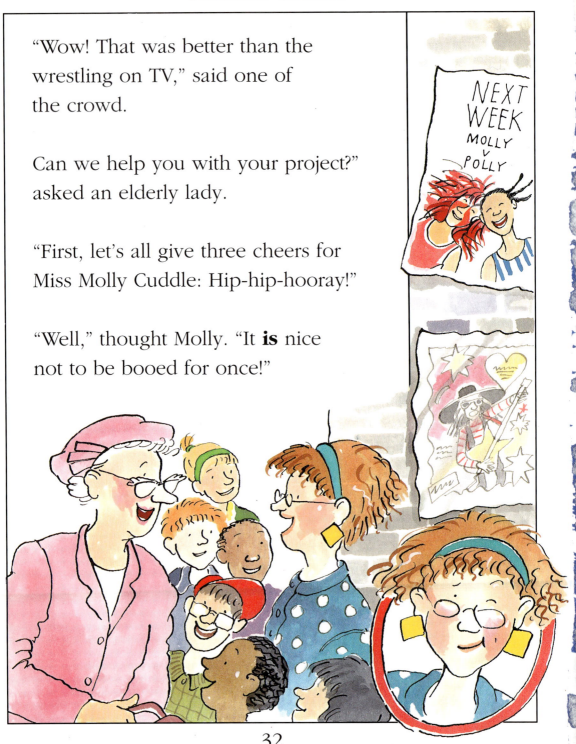